MW01595581

Are You Listening?

Are You Listening?

KELLY WICKENS

Pleasant Word
A Division of WINEPRESS PUBLISHING

© 2007 by Kelly Wickens. All rights reserved.

A special thank you to Carrie Little
Author photo by Maria Hey @mariaheyphotography.com

Pleasant Word (a division of WinePress Publishing, PO Box 428, Enumclaw, WA 98022) functions only as book publisher. As such, the ultimate design, content, editorial accuracy, and views expressed or implied in this work are those of the author.

No part of this publication may be reproduced, stored in a retrieval system, or transmitted in any way by any means—electronic, mechanical, photocopy, recording, or otherwise—without the prior permission of the copyright holder, except as provided by USA copyright law.

Unless otherwise noted, all Scripture references are taken from the Holy Bible, New International Version, Copyright © 1973, 1978, 1984 by the International Bible Society. Used by permission of Zondervan Publishing House. The "NIV" and "New International Version" trademarks are registered in the United States Patent and Trademark Office by International Bible Society.

Scripture references marked KJV are taken from the King James Version of the Bible.

Scripture references marked NASB are taken from the New American Standard Bible, © 1960, 1963, 1968, 1971, 1972, 1973, 1975, 1977 by The Lockman Foundation. Used by permission.

ISBN 13: 978-1-4141-0937-4
ISBN 10: 1-4141-0937-7
Library of Congress Catalog Card Number: 2007900030

I dedicate this book especially to my Kloey Grace,
also to the earthly angels who walked
through the valley with me.

Love, to Jim and Kasey
and
A special thanks to Kerby,
who allowed me to breathe again.

Introduction:

Are You Listening?

Are you listening? That is the question. God is speaking to us. He is trying to reach us. Sometimes His ways are subtle, nudging ways. But sometimes He has to get out the big megaphone to get our attention. I have imagined what that figurative megaphone must look like. I know it exists because He has used it on me. Yes, God is speaking to you and He will get your attention one way or another. Maybe He is revealing part of His plan to you. Maybe He is channeling your talents and gifts to use them as He intended.

We will be delivered to heaven on the wings of His grace with effortless surrendering and humbling of ourselves before Him. We can be blessed by His sovereignty and the glory of His grace.

Yet, don't miss out on what He has to show you. He really wants your attention one way or another. Beth Moore, one of my favorite women's Bible study authors declared, "You don't want to take a field trip to learn this lesson." Do we often hear but not listen, or listen and ignore? Enjoy the security that only a personal relationship with our Lord can offer. I feel the earthly value of our salvation is increased by the amount of Christian maturation that takes place while we are alive on earth.

I would like to share my story about how God spoke to me and prepared me for a defining moment in my life. God took me from a place of casual Christianity to a place of joy that can only come from Him. A good story has a beginning, middle, and end but with me it rarely comes in that order. I consider you prepared. So away we go!

Chapter 1

Jesus said, "Let the little children come to me, and do not hinder them, for the kingdom of heaven belongs to such as these."

—Matthew 19:14

I will not say that 2000 was a bad year. It was actually very nice until November 12. Actually, November 12 was a very fine day until 5:30 that Sunday evening. But if I were to be asked what the worst day of my life was, it would be Monday, November 13, 2000.

The first task I was faced with that day was to tell my four-year-old daughter that her little sister was so badly hurt that the doctors could not help her. Kloey Grace would be living in heaven now. We would not see her again until we get to heaven ourselves.

The previous evening Kasey, Kloey (21 months and 2 days), their daddy, and a friend, Brian, were playing Twister in the living room. I was in the kitchen, checking an item for a Christmas gift in the JC Penney catalog, while my King Ranch Chicken baked in the oven. I could hear wonderful sounds of laughter from the living room as Jim spun out commands that were twisting everyone into knots: "Right foot red, left hand yellow!" Yahoo! Everyone was having a blast and acting goofy. Kloey excitedly ran out of the living room and headed to the front entry area of our home. The moment to follow changed my life forever. Kloey must have pulled down or hung on the glass table top of a concrete-base pedestal table that was in the center of that room. Time had apparently weakened the integrity of the cement glue that was holding the two parts of the base together. The Base was a birdbath with a bowl and a stand topped with a thick piece of round beveled glass, all connected by cement glue. In description, it sounds like a hazard, but we had become complacent with it being in our home as it had been there since before we even thought of having children. Like sin, the more you are exposed to it the less you see wrong with it and we just get used to it in our lives. Anyway, with the weight of Kloey unbalancing the piece, it toppled.

Responding to the noise, I was in the room in a second to find Kloey pinned under the heavy bowl part of the pedestal that was the birdbath. With my adrenalin flowing, I was easily able to toss the concrete bowl off her. When Jim came into the room, he thought she had just gotten the air knocked out of her; he didn't realize the heavy bowl had been on top of her. Kloey had no visible injuries. I looked hard into her eyes, which turned out to be last time I did so. Her silence and her eyes told me something only a mother can know.

"I'm calling 911. She's not right." Jim was holding her. I ran from house to house to seek immediate help from neighbors. I am not sure what I thought anyone else would be able to do, but at that moment, while waiting for the professionals, the "Martha" in me made me feel the need to do something. I was running between neighbors' houses and redialing my call to 911, as it seemed like more time had passed than what actually had.

Jim was out on the front porch when he yelled, "I'm losing her, Kel. I'm losing her!"

His words were repeated over and over. Our neighbor Barry escorted me back across the street as I told him the situation. He and Jim attempted mouth-to-mouth resuscitation as I relayed instructions from the 911 operator.

I was later told that all the mouth-to-mouth and any other medical attention—even if EMS had been standing on our front porch at the time of the accident—could not have prevented the outcome. Knowing this today, I so wish I would have been like busy Martha's sister, Mary, and just held Kloey in my arms and told her how much we all loved her, how we prayed for her to be a part of our family even before her conception. I would have told her bye-bye just for now, but that we would see her again when Jesus called us to heaven. As it was, though, God puts in a mother's heart to try to fix her children's hurts. As I see it now He was also protecting me from the visions of which Kloey's daddy has ownership.

Having your child's life slip from her while in your arms…I have no words for that, but among other things it provides great ammunition for the Devil. It is a struggle not to allow Satan to replay the video in your mind. Satan loves to take horrible images of life and play them over again in those quiet times. This is one of his oldest tricks to rob Christians of their joy.

As the event played out, Brian's mom was notified to come get him, and the ambulance arrived and called for air life. Our neighbors, the Pattersons, ushered Kasey, who had been with her friend Brain in the car waiting further instructions, down to their house, where she ended up spending the night. Barry, Jim, and the EMS crew were inside with Kloey. I was "out of the way" at the bottom of the front porch stairs. Brian's mom, Denise, had stayed to pray over me. I had heard about the power of prayer so much that it had become cliché. But at this moment of unparalleled urgency for answered prayer, my desperate plea seemed as if it was reaching the heavens with the intensity that it was leaving my lips. The weather was suddenly and strangely changing.

Chapter 1

The storm that had just hit my life was shooting up to the skies. I was in a crisis and I knew the heavens knew it too. When I get to heaven I am going to ask what was going on in the heavens at that moment. The skies darkened, the wind dramatically kicked up, and the temperature dropped. I thought of the accounts I had seen and heard of the storm that arose when Jesus took His last breath on the cross.

The air-life helicopter crew had planned to land in front of our house, but because of the very recent change in the winds, they were not able to drop down safely in a tight space. They landed at the nearby golf driving range, and when they thought they had Kloey stable enough, the ambulance took her to the helicopter and then on to University Hospital.

I still hear the sound of the helicopter hovering in hopes of landing. I still hear the sound of the helicopter making an alternate plan. When I hear a helicopter now, it brings me back. I pray, "Lord, if that is an air-life I hear, please allow the medics to do your will, Lord, and be with the family as they do."

The emergency crew did not allow Jim to ride in the chopper with Kloey. The ambulance took him to the hospital. I think now I know why they didn't allow him to go. I think they realized the seriousness of her injury. She had never been conscious since Jim lost her, although they said she let out a cry when I was at the bottom of the porch. My neighbors took me in a car. We converged on the hospital not long after Kloey did.

The emergency room gave us a small private room for us and a caravan of friends that miraculously appeared. We waited for the news of the doctors' assessment, but the wait was short. The news was beyond comprehension. Most or maybe all of my world became a blur as all the friends left the room to let us have privacy. My body went limp and I slid down in the seat. I don't believe I had a sound to give at that moment, but I could hear clearly no other sound but my husband weeping from a place inside him that produced a cry of loss and sadness that I never want to hear again—the sob of death.

"I want to see her. I want to be with her," I whispered to the nurse who had her arms around me. I began to move out of the room as if I knew right where to go in a hall of many closed doors.

"We'll move her to a room were you can go be with her, but right now she's not in a place you can go," she explained.

My eyes were sealed shut in an escape mode. I heard Jim from behind his tears ask, "Is she here or is she gone?" Literally, the news had been incomprehensible. He was still trying to wrap his mind around what we had been told. I guess we all were, and I had to see for myself.

The nurse was ready to walk us to see Kloey. When I cracked open my eyes for the first time, I saw the face of the nurse who had been sitting with her arm around me. I expected to see a professional that dealt with like situations on a daily basis. University Hospital is a unit that receives the worst of all accidents. Instead the nurse had a sweet face with a steady stream of tears flowing from her eyes. She was trying to control them with a tissue. I was in such shock, I suppose. Somehow this struck my heart that she, the professional, was not hardened, but deeply affected. Her face was my visual of the reality I would see shortly.

We moved to the room the staff had prepared for us. This is where we spent the rest of the evening with our pastor, close friends and Kloey's body. I embraced her body for hours, until her smell was gone. The warmth had left her skin, and her body, still supporting her baby fat, had grown stiff.

We had made the decision to donate her organs, but given the unknown circumstances of her internal injuries and her young age, only her beautiful cornea were taken. "The eyes are the windows to the soul." The surgical teams were assembled, as the operation had to be done in a timely manner. Shortly after 1:00 A.M., they covered my baby's head with a sheet and wheeled her down the hall and beyond two swinging sterile double doors, beyond which I was not allowed to pass. Even though those double doors had no lock on them—they did not even have a latch—yet they exuded the finality and impassability of prison walls. The doors were daunting, and I was not able to pass through those swinging gates at that time, but there will be a time when I will be able to pass through some beautiful gates to reunite with my Bitsy Boo, my Kloey.

Our family has a policy to keep Kloey's sweet memories ever present. Friends are made welcome to help us recall any little ditties about Kloey. She is present in our conversations, our home, and above all our spiritual life, as we owe the relationship we have with our Lord today to what He had to take from us that day in November 2000. It is obvious to all that Satan has no victory here. We have a faith stronger than before. The Devil is not allowed, in the name of Jesus, to rob us of the short time we had with our precious daughter Kloey Grace Wickens.

This is the beginning of my story. As far as the rest of my story, I will refer to these hours surrounding the accident as my defining moment.

Chapter 2

Now we see but a poor reflection as in a mirror; then we shall see face to face. Now I know in part; then I shall know fully, even as I am fully known.

—1 Corinthians 13:12

Today as I write, Kloey has been away from me for three years, seven months, and five days. Today I no longer feel that my defining moment defines me. I don't feel that I am "the lady who lost the child" or "the lady whose daughter was killed."

It has taken three-and-a-half years to get to this place. To illustrate: At one time my desk was scattered with papers. Each paper represented a memory of Kloey. The good ones were there as well as the bad, horrifying ones. Each day I sat at my desk those papers were in full view, not only surrounding my space, but engulfing it. Today, I still take ownership of all those papers, but they are filed away in the drawer. I can pull them out at any time, but they have a place and they don't consume me. There is no need to feel sad for me. I am one of those blessed ones who "gets it" now.

God truly does use the bad for good. I have these words framed in my home: "At the loss of a child, find comfort in the sovereignty of God. There is no lost potential, no purpose unaccomplished; there is only the glorious plan of God perfectly fulfilled in a precious little life." I don't know who authored that, but I thank them. This was one of nearly four hundred cards and letters we received after our defining moment.

Most of the cards were sent from friends and family. Some were from folks we barely knew, and a few were from people we had never met, but who were truly saddened by the situation. When reading their words, I could feel them clinging to their kids and praying that they would never know our grief. Others who had lost someone dear to them were saying to me that they knew my grief. I believe they did. Only those who have lost a child can know the deep hole of grief we had entered. The others who told me they knew how I felt, if they so dared to choose those words, were only lying.

I know too that not everyone is able to get out of that deep hole of grief. It is only by God's mighty hands pulling us from that deep dark place that we walk among you now. Ah, "the glorious plan of God perfectly fulfilled." I pass by those words many times every day, and every day they inspire me. Those words make it easy for me to surrender to God. I can testify that He is driving my bus! It is not our calling to know His plan now, but as His Word indicates, someday we will understand fully.

Back when the pain was so fresh, I would try to go about my day, run my errands, get Kasey back to whatever normal was going to be now. I remember an encounter I had at Mailboxes-R-Us down the street from our house as I went to mail a Christmas gift.

"I heard about your daughter and I'm so sorry. I don't know how you can be out and about…I don't know how you do it!"

"I owe it to the Lord," I told her.

She replied," Okaaay…" as she turned away.

Lots of people, even if they didn't know me, knew of my situation, and I felt like everyone was watching me to see how I was handling the grief. I did try to put my best foot forward when I was around others, but when I was alone I wept. I would think about what a beautiful place Kloey was in and how I would like to be with her and what measures I might take to get there. The Lord assured me He and His angels were taking care of her. The Lord also reminded me how much Kasey needed me with her and that He had some plans for me in this world. I didn't let myself be alone too much.

Because of the ever-present lump in my throat, I was not able to articulate at that time to the Mailboxes-R-Us lady what was in my heart and what I thought of her patronizing indignation of disbelief. I knew I would have to get better because God wanted me to be a testimony to what He was doing in my life. I felt called to give voice to the Lord. The next time, I was going to be strong enough to tell folks how God was pulling me from that deep dark hole of grief and that anyone who would grab on to His mighty hands could be pulled from whatever hole they had dug for themselves or had been thrust into unexpectedly. Yes, God was speaking to me, and I was listening more closely than ever.

I feel so empowered since my defining moment. The worst fear any mother could have, happened to me. Nothing else could ever happen that could be as bad. So when the worst has already happened, you feel free to live the rest of your life more fearlessly. At first, I think I challenged God a bit with things like pulling out aggressively into traffic, crossing the street without looking, and a few other silly things. I felt like I had just as much invested in heaven as I did on earth. *Whatever will be, will be.* I sure felt a total surrendering to God. *Nothing I can do about it anyway,* I thought. *I have no control here.* I can't tell you how freeing it was to relinquish all control.

As I write today, I would be remiss not to say my behavior was not wise. God also blesses us with common sense to make good choices, and it honors Him if we use that good sense. Maybe I don't challenge God anymore and I'm not so sure what that phase was all about, but I still feel a sense of empowerment. Yes, I do regret that God had to use His big megaphone to get my attention. The giant alarm clock went off, He took me on a field trip, or whatever metaphor comes to your mind. I am listening now! He is the great teacher. When He takes you through the fire, you will undoubtedly be changed and your new life will be defined at that moment. He strengthens your faith as He walks through the fire with you.

The walk through the fiery furnace was bittersweet for me. The loss of my sweet baby Kloey was horrific indeed, but my spiritual encounters and faith-building journey was and still is a revelation of life-defining proportions. Good does come from bad if your heart is with the Holy One. I'm not sure of any other way to fully gain understanding of God's presence if it is not to go with Him on a field trip of such magnitude. Fear not if He chooses to take you on a field trip, because once through the pain, grief, and suffering, on the other side await great rewards.

So I ask you again, are you listening? What's He saying to you? For now we see through only a dull mirror, but only in His time will we see clearly. My message to you: Don't wait for the ultimate wake-up call from God. *Wake up now and grow in the Lord!*

Chapter 3

So I also will choose harsh treatment for them and will bring upon them what they dread. For when I called, no one answered, when I spoke, no one listened. They did evil in my sight and chose what displeases me.

—Isaiah 66:4

None of us, however young or old, knows how long we have on earth. That's why it is so important to fulfill our duties as God calls. God does not live in a faraway place beyond outer space, above the clouds, trillions of miles beyond. Heaven is closer than you think. Heaven is only a breath away. God lives at our fingertips. Swat your hand in the air only as far as you can reach and you may have just grazed an angel!

Kasey asked her Bible study teacher, "How big is God?" She replied, "God is so big He can hold the whole world in His hands, and He is tiny enough to fit in your heart." He is our God, a God more powerful than our human minds can wrap around. God is everywhere as He uses all things to reach and teach us. Everything and everyone is at His disposal and can be used as His tool at any time He deems. I pray that all my readers will have an increased awareness of the God surrounding them and a deepened spiritual perspective on all events, minor to major.

Now is the time to begin growing in your relationship with God. Take the time to listen to what God is laying on your heart. The Lord has put on my heart stories to share with you not just to tell you about the grief I experienced in losing Kloey or the details of my particular defining moment, but to help you find your defining moment. My spiritual growth and increased spiritual awareness were prompted by a loss of life so precious to me. I hope you can use my defining moment as an illustration to inspire you spiritually. I pray that your defining moment will be as painless as reading someone else's testimony, but as memorable as God intends. Certainly, I am not through growing and maturing. If you think you are, you have further to go than any of us.

The next few short chapters will be personal accounts of divine intervention; times I truly felt the Holy

Spirit was using His "tools" to reach me. In the present it is sometimes difficult to clearly interpret what God means. Often it is not until that all-powerful hindsight comes to be that our little human brains can understand. I believe that as we practice listening to God, opening our hearts to Him fully, and being quiet in His presence, only then can we best see the vision He sends to us on a personal level. I pray for you now that God will increase your awareness of His glorious presence. I challenge you to start practicing *now*!

Because I had hit that magic number of age thirty-five and had a baby growing inside me, my doctor suggested I get an amniocentesis. Doctors use this process to screen for genetic disorders by inserting a very long needle into the sac where the baby is growing and extract amniotic fluid. There is a risk, since the needle is inserted so close to the baby. My whole pregnancy process had been quite scientifically based, so I didn't question one more test; nor did I make a big deal of it. It wasn't until a girlfriend asked me to do something with her.

"I can't tomorrow. I have my amnio." I could tell she was shocked that this was the first she had heard about it.

"Is Jim going with you?"

"Of course not, he's working."

She quizzed me. "Well, if Jim isn't going with you, who is?"

It wasn't until she spoke those words that I began to wonder why I needed someone to go with me. I dismissed her and told her I would be fine. What I should have told her was that I would not be alone because Jesus would be there with me.

The next day, the day of my appointment, I thought no more about our conversation.

After a consultation time, the process began in a small, dimly lit exam room, which made the sonogram machine clearer. There was that big needle and a brighter light so the doctor could see where he needed to put that needle. There was the sweet nurse, too, who spoke in a calming voice. The certainty of their actions assured me that they had done this procedure hundreds of times. I closed my eyes in prayer for good results from this test. There went the cold gel on my tummy that is used to glide the sonogram wand. I felt the doctor's hands on my tummy to feel where Kloey was. Soon I felt the needle being inserted.

But wait! Who was this? Whose hand was this? I felt another hand on my tummy on my left side. The doctor was on the right with his two hands. Out of reflex, I darted my eyes to the nurse who I felt sure was still standing by the sonogram machine. Yes, she was still there. I knew whose hand I had felt on my tummy. I did not go to that appointment alone.

The Lord was with Kloey from the beginning of her life just as He was at the end and remains with her today in eternity. "As you do not know the path of the wind, or how the body is formed in a mother's womb, so you cannot understand the work of God, the Maker of all things" (Eccl. 11:5).

Clearly, the Lord spoke to me on the Tuesday night after Kloey had left us on Sunday. Tugging and urging me in the middle of the night, the Lord brought me to the computer and He told me to write. Once I was there He told me *what* to write. He needed me to speak at the service on Thursday. I was at the bottom of a hole of grief. I was desperate for answers. I had no choice but to be like play dough. "Because I am weak, I am strong in Christ." Unfortunately, that is often a statement that is only truly evident in our lives when we are in a crisis mode. However, if we can commit to that every moment of the day, what peace we would have! I will say it again: *When we are the weakest in ourselves is when we are the strongest in the Lord.* I had no choice but to be obedient.

At 3:00 A.M. He not only showed me what I needed to deliver at the service, but He put into perspective a gift that Kloey had given us. Through our grief and our testimony of faith, I had an opportunity to witness for the Lord and provide evidence of His power. I was able to do so in her eulogy, titled "Kloey's Gift."

Remembering what I know to be true, it is not that I must understand, but I must be obedient to the Lord. I share with you my notes that the Lord spilled out on my computer that early morning. I am glad I listened, because my words touched many at the service and brought them closer to the Lord. In a case or two, they met with the Lord for the first time.

KLOEY'S GIFT

The Holy Spirit is working within me to give me strength to come forth and speak today. It is true that there is no greater pain than that of a mother who has lost her child. Just like you, I have asked why God took our sweet baby Kloey Grace, my little Bitsy Boo. Those who knew her well knew she truly was an angel on earth who was too good for this place.

Hear me as I speak. Both of our daughters are miracle babies—truly gifts from God above. They were conceived in the fertility clinic using procedures called in vitro fertilization. The Lord's hand was present throughout this process. My babies are a precious gift to me. As I look back, I can see the Lord had been strengthening my faith, not just to deal with this tragedy, but to come before you today to share with you the purpose God had for Kloey.

I am called to deliver a message of salvation to all in this place so the passing of my sweet child from this earth will not be a useless act of suffering. No, I did not want to be the example for you today, but now I must tell you. The only way to heaven and eternal life, to be delivered from the pit of hell, is by opening your heart to Jesus, asking Him to come into your life, and living your life as intended in the Scriptures. Some of you will leave this earth before I do. Kloey and I are asking that you pray for salvation so you will spend your eternity in heaven. When you get there, hold Kloey and rock her for me. Kloey needs you there, and I want you there too. Let us honor Kloey.

Indeed, Kloey delivered us all a gift—the ultimate gift.

Chapter 4

> "See that you don't look down on one of these little ones. For I tell you that their angels in heaven always see the face of my Father in heaven."
>
> —Matthew 18:10

From the time a mother holds her baby for the first time, she knows the child is special. There is that indescribable connection that makes you feel that you have known each other all your life. Those who have children will certainly recall that "aha" moment that you say to yourself, "So you're the one I've been waiting for!" "It's nice to finally see what you look like."

With Kloey Grace I experienced a much more poignant occasion. I was overcome with a sensation that she was special beyond just the natural "mommy thinks so" way. I describe the sensation to be a supernatural, spiritually special kind. Kloey was less than a month old. Sleeping in the frilly white bassinet beside our bed, she woke me with her cooing.

Kloey never gave me too much notice before she escalated into a full-blown cry. I tried to keep reasonably quiet for working Dad sleeping soundly beside me. My routine for the two o'clock feeding was to run to the bathroom and splash a little water on my face before I began nursing. I bolted out of bed and scurried past the bassinet. Whoa! I felt electricity and energy over the bassinet. I saw two sphere-like forms hovering only for a fraction of a second. It was like they came in secret and had gotten caught by a human eye. I hesitated in the bathroom to absorb this heart-stopping occurrence. I had a feeling like I had never had before. It was such a moment that there was no doubt that I had encountered something very huge, beyond human comprehension and well beyond this world.

I know. Even through unfailing faith, knowing the Lord can do all things, and believing that God's angels are everywhere, it still sounds crazy.

Remembering my purpose for being up in the first place, I approached the bassinet to find Kloey peacefully asleep. I glanced at the clock to find it was nowhere near the predictable two o'clock feeding time. Exactly who or what had she been visiting? Or, rather, who had been visiting her? I believe it was a friendly conversation because I recall her coos being happy sounds. I felt a bit honored in receiving a visit from something from the heavens. I believe Kloey was cooing and communicating with these beings. Since she seemed to be at peace and comforted by them, I was not frightened at all, just very curious.

I checked out a few books in the public library on angels and the like. I also referred to passages in the Bible pertaining to angelic or supernatural encounters. I read that it is believed that children have two guardian angels assigned to them while they sleep. Is that what I witnessed?

Today, my heart tells me they were angels sent as messengers from God to deliver to Kloey Grace something God wanted her to know. I am no scholar or prophet, so I can't testify to their true purpose and I don't think any book from the library would have the answer either. Yet knowing the word *angel* itself comes from the Greek word *messenger*, I am certain in my heart as the day is long that they were delivering a message to Kloey that early February morning.

The way Kloey lived her short life is compelling evidence that she knew she would only have a short time to make a huge impact. She lived totally vivaciously as to absorb and experience what life had to offer a little one.

What a nice lesson she taught us, as none of us knows when our time to depart will be. Will we have regrets when we leave? Will we have neglected to know Jesus in a personal way? Friends, we are all going to die; it's the "when" that no one is sure of. Live like you are going to die tomorrow…you may.

Kloey trick-or-treated like there would be no next time. Everyone laughed at her relentlessness. She made sure she was in every picture and wanted a few extra taken when everyone else was ready to move on. Photographers I did not know, professional and amateur, felt drawn to take her picture. I am glad for this, as I have some unexpected gifts after Kloey had left us. Volunteers in the church nursery would comment on their attraction to Kloey. Statistically, she did everything with a little more vigor and sooner and quicker than the average baby. I could go on citing examples, but I think the message is clear. Maybe Kloey did have a small insight into the Lord's perfect plan. The Bible tells me that Jesus knew His death was of God's plan and the time was near. It's fun when you can catch a glimpse of what the Lord has in store for you, but He so often keeps the details top secret. I say to you, don't put off the things you want to do and certainly don't put off your salvation!

So what did I do with this revelation I experienced during the night? I told my husband what had happened. After saying it out loud once, I realized it sounded like some freaky post-partum ghost story from a sleep-deprived woman who was on the edge of only the Lord knows what. I kept quiet, but in my heart I new Kloey had been visited.

Approximately nine months later I shared my story with my mom and sister while they were visiting from West Texas. We were sitting in the same room where the incident had occurred, and I gestured toward the frilly white bassinet. They were attentive to my story, and, much to my surprise, they did not dismiss the possibility of my theory. They did not roll their eyes or do that sideways-look thing to each other. Instead Mom said, "We'll be sure to watch the rest of Kloey's life to see if there may be more signs of a gift of communication with the spiritual world." "The rest of her life," she said. How ironic that the rest of her life was such a short time.

The next time I shared this story was the night of my defining moment. I shared it with my pastor, Malcom McQueen, as we leaned over Kloey's lifeless body. He spoke of it again to the congregation at Kloey's memorial service. I don't think many could wrap their minds around what Pastor Malcolm was relaying, much less follow its meaning as I saw it. It's truly one of those "you had to be there" moments. No one will be as sincerely impacted by it as I was.

I close this chapter with a thought for all of you thinking you will never encounter an angel. They have the ability to take on many forms. It is not how many wings they have, what grandeur they impose, or the shape they have. They are angels because of what they *do*. You may have entertained angels unaware!

Chapter 5

It is my pleasure to tell you about the miraculous signs and wonders that the Most High has performed for me.

—Daniel 4:2

Jim and I were Christians. I understood and received God's promise of heaven in the fifth grade, and Jim was born again in Christ as an adult just before we met. We were growing slowly in the Word. We were married and worshipped in a small Presbyterian church. We were active participants there at John Calvin. We were senior high youth group leaders before we had kids of our own. Then I became the nursery coordinator. I served on the building committee. We volunteered for this and that.

Jim and I hardly ever missed our Sunday school class. Yet our lives were not fully led by the Holy Spirit.

Jim was traveling a lot. He always had, but now that we had two girls it seemed to matter more. Jim quit his profession as a civil engineer acting as project manager for a company where he was erecting mining equipment. He and his buddy, Dave, were going to be day-traders in our bull stock market. It was agreed that if Dave reached a certain profit level Jim would join him at the trading house full time. That happened in May 2000. What a leap of faith! The stock market was unpredictable—that is a given. Besides, there were already signs of the bull leaving town. But what a lifestyle it offered. Jim's day no longer started at 5:30 A.M. He took Kasey to school and was home in the afternoon soon after she was. Sometimes he would finish up midmorning and be home before Kloey and I had barely started our day. He wore shorts and T-shirts to work, a certain plus for any man.

The Lord was blessing us financially as well. Jim was making his hobby work for him. Kloey benefited in that she did not know a time when Daddy had to go out of town. It always took Kasey a day or two to warm up to Dad if he had been away for several days. We didn't realize at the time what a divine intervention this new plan was.

During the course of praying about this new lifestyle change, we had humbled ourselves to God and had begun the process of allowing the Holy Spirit to guide our ways. At that time, I don't think we were aware of the Christian vocabulary to describe what was happening in us. Nevertheless, we were letting go and letting God.

Yes, let go and let God. Wow, we didn't know how those words were about to impact our way of life. That was just what our routine, religious life was missing. Just that very word, *religious*, meant something different to me. It indeed meant routine. It meant legalism. Religion had nothing to do with having faith in the Lord and worshipping Him on a personal level. The Most High tore the curtain in the temple long ago as a symbol of His desire that we have a direct relationship with Him. He desires us to have conversations (pray) directly to Him and no other! In turn, He speaks directly to us, like any other personal relationship we have. Don't miss out on this relationship a minute longer. Receive His Holy Spirit. "Religion" conveyed nothing to me about the lessons I was going to learn about His sovereignty and omniscience.

Jim was able to drink up every possible minute with Kloey. Our new free-spirited lifestyle was a step out for conservative folk like us. We could not imagine ourselves doing something so drastic where our livelihood was at stake, especially when Jim had such a thriving career. This was the first step God took to bond Jim and Kloey together like they never could have been; given the short twenty-one months she was to be here. Yes, God began to prepare us for what was to come. Jim was given this gift of time with his baby daughter.

Jim day traded for exactly one year, from May to May. Not only was God filling him up with Kloey and Kasey, but the Lord was filling Jim with His Word. Making the most of this uncommitted time, Jim read the Bible from cover to cover! In doing so, Jim was able to understand the conclusive word of the Lord, the total picture. This is an accomplishment I myself cannot boast. Jim tells me there is little room for interpretation when you have read both the Old and New Testaments and treat the Bible as a whole. He had made me understand how plucking verses out here and there could be confusing or misinterpreted. The Bible in its entirety leaves no doubt of God's big picture and His desires. I relied on my sweet husband for many things, but because God had given Jim the wisdom of His Word, I depended much on him for his special insight. I think we were able to see things more clearly because of Jim's total read-through and his willingness to teach and share with me during our grief.

I probably don't have to point out the obvious, but it gives me joy to give God His glory. It was no coincidence Jim read the Bible during those months. Jim could have chosen to read a good fiction bestseller, played some golf, or taken a nap, by golly! Jim made this choice to read the Bible because God needed him to know and receive the Holy Word and be the best spiritual leader of the family he could be in the months to follow and for all times.

God's calendar has events in each of our lives that are firmly decided by God, and there is nothing we can do about it. Just as Scripture is full of prophecy, God's ways with us each day can be a prophecy of what's on that calendar. Let God have His way with you.

Chapter 6

Keep watch over yourselves and all the flock of which the Holy Spirit has made you overseers. Be shepherds of the church of God, which he bought with his own blood.

—Acts 20:28

As I mentioned, we were active in our little church where we had been married in 1988. It was the only church we had attended as a married couple. I came home after working in the nursery one Sunday morning with some news for Jim. "God has told me we need to find a new church. Not when Kasey gets older or when I finish my duty as nursery director, but *now*." Jim trusted me in that he too was strong enough in his faith that he knew we did not have a choice but to be obedient. Jim also believed in my relationship with our God to rely on what I was testifying to him.

In Sept 1999, we spoke with Pastor Malcolm about our decision to leave the church. Everyone understood the logistic reasons and was not surprised. We had moved, and our drive had been some distance for about 5 years now. Kasey was the only kid her age in the church, and it was no secret she was not being nurtured to full capacity at this church. I trained a replacement for nursery director and prepared to leave the faces I saw every Sunday. No one at John Calvin Presbyterian Church, including us, saw clearly the reason for the push God gave us to another church home.

We began visiting other churches.

In January 2000, God put us at a church with lots of young families or, as in our case, families with young children. Most of the two thousand plus members were in the same stage of life and on the same page that we were. It was a Spirit-filled church. In plain talk, it was a growing, moving, and shakin' place! At first it seemed a little out there, because I was so used to the quiet reverence and traditions of the Presbyterians. I grew to love it. Hey, these people worshipped the Lord! We became involved in an amazing Sunday school class in September and a small group in October. Suddenly, the church seemed to shrink for us as we began developing relationships.

I know now that this was our support group that God had put into place for us. My small group leaders were the first phone call I made after I called 911 on the day of my defining moment, even though I had met them only one month prior. The Lord told me they were going to pray me through this crisis. What a crisis it turned out to be. Truly, the group, the church, lifted us up to the Lord in prayer in numbers that could be felt as a physical covering.

I had an opportunity to gather with some who had been covering me in prayer. I wanted to tell them their prayers had made a difference. I wanted to convey what it felt like to be receiving the blessings from so many prayers. I needed them to know, though I had no words for them that would make the impact on them. I needed a visual! I gathered them into a circle around a large blanket and asked them to hold on to an edge of the blanket. I placed a water balloon in the middle of the blanket. As I spoke to them about what they had done for me and how they had brought me to the place where I could be there, the balloon jostled and rolled around dangerously on the blanket, but it didn't fall and it didn't break. You see, the balloon was me, and the blanket was their support in prayer.

To continue my visual explanation, I took the blanket away. This time the balloon fell to the ground and did what water balloons do. I would have surely had the same fate as the water balloon had it not been for my faith and the faith of many prayer warriors. As the Old Testament describes the symbolic ritual of burning incense as a visual of prayers rising to heaven, I was lifted in as real a way as the smoke from the incense arose.

Many different communities prayed for us, as the tragedy of a death of a child touches many. Most did not know me or my family, but they knew God. Because of this support system I felt God's grace, His sovereignty, His perfect plan at work, His glory, and His omniscience. I discovered that happiness comes from a circumstance, but joy comes from the Lord. Even in the worst of conditions, I can still have joy through the Lord. "May peace and joy be yours" used to be just something inside a Christmas card, but now it is the most personal and perfect prayer I can have for another. As hard as it was to leave our comfortable little church, I am thankful I was obedient to the Lord. I listened. I felt that little tap on my shoulder from one of those angels assigned to deal with us.

There is a story in Genesis 21. Hagar is in the desert with her dying son, Ishmael, in serious need of water. "Then God opened her eyes and she saw a well of water" (Gen. 21:19). Sometimes God may bring you to the "well." Often He will even bring the "well" to you. In either case, be prepared to drink! Sure, I have moments when God is showing me something. I truly know He is, but I don't know what message He is trying to convey. I

Chapter 6

pray for revelation and wisdom. Then, I listen. I know it's me He is using for His plan. I am His holy vessel! I am the one! Ask Him, "What can I do for You?" And then say, "Yes, Lord!"

Chapter 7

He who listens to a life-giving rebuke will be at home among the wise.

—Proverbs 15:31

I had heard about the women's retreat in Sunday school. I didn't know any of the apparently two hundred women who were going. Accommodations were four to a room with a bed partner.

God told me to sign up and pay my fee. I was obedient even though I had never, I mean never, been away from my girls overnight. I look back now and say, "Wow! That was pretty independent of me!" The week before the retreat Jim confirmed what I was sure to be true. "You have no clue how to take care of my girls for a weekend!" Of course, that was Satan putting lies and doubt into my head, because intellectually I know Jim is one of the best dads around. But Jim had done something that I would not have approved of letting the girls do, so that was it! I could not leave them!

I called the retreat registration person and told her tearfully, "I just can't leave my girls, so please fill my spot with the next name on the waiting list." She could have said OK, but do you know what she said? "Why don't you pray about it over the weekend, and if you still feel the same on Monday I'll do what you ask." I agreed. Was she another one of those crazy angels taking shape on a phone line?

Satan did not win this one! Not only did I go to the retreat, but God spoke to me personally. I became so much more dedicated to my relationship with God. It turned out to be a good thing that I didn't know anyone, because I got to better know an old friend, Jesus. He talked to me about being a mom and what He expected of me as far as making disciples of the two human gifts that I'd been given.

God specifically spoke to me about my youngest, Kloey Grace. "Watch her sleep, smell her smell, photograph her moves in your mind and record her voice in your head," the Lord told me. I thought this to be good advice to any mom, since children grow up so fast. I knew she was going to be my last baby, so I better enjoy this special time with vigor.

With my firstborn I thought every stage was a permanent way of life. There would be no end to nursing or toting that heavy baby carrier. Wow! How fast one phase leaves and another begins! When we're in the child-raising phase of life the days seem to never end. Yet the years fly by like leaves in the wind. My girls were conceived in the fertility clinic by invitro fertilization, but as Oprah says, "That's another show." Anyway, we were sure this was our last chance to enjoy the toddler stage.

"Yes, Lord, I know now from experience that the moments spent when they're little are fleeting ones. Thanks for reminding me." I began to pause and enjoy the routine occurrences and focus more on Kloey's ways. I memorized how she looked sleeping and the scent of her little "girliness." I made those mental notes the Lord challenged me to make, but also took lots of video and pictures that sometimes the second time around parents get lax about. I even took a picture of Kloey eating cereal that morning of November 12, 2000. I treasure that picture now and note that it was a "God thing" that I would take a picture of something so routine on a morning we were bustling off to church. She left us for eternity that very evening.

I know now that the message God was sending to me was that He would be taking her soon and not because she would be on the fast track to preadolescence. I thank my all-knowing Father for the awareness that was

Chapter 7

breathed into me. That last month of precious memories might have breezed by in the course of being a busy mommy. God is good. I'm glad I listened.

Chapter 8

"I am the true vine, and my Father is the true gardener. He cuts off every branch in me that bears no fruit, while every branch that bears fruit he prunes so that it will be even more fruitful."

—John 15:1

It's a process. The Lord continues to reveal things to me. That is what gets me through everything now. Today, as I write, it is the fourth anniversary of my defining moment. What does this day mean to me? What should it mean? It's another day on the calendar. I give it no power over me other than it is that day on the calendar that changed my life forever. On Kloey's birthday on February 10, we plant rosebushes in a corner of our backyard that we have identified as her memorial garden. The rose is the flower of February and represents passion. Our roses are of the dom de'coure variety. They are red for the blood of Jesus and fragrant to symbolize how we need to be in Christ. Today, I picked the beautifully blooming roses just as God picked Kloey off this earth on this same day four years ago. He prunes us all. Doing this task without gloves allows me to feel pain from their thorns just as pain is felt when we are being pruned by the Lord.

Much pain came from the thoughts I had of letting Kloey down. After all, I was her mother. It was my job to protect her, keep her safe, and nurture her well-being. I was responsible for the fatal table being in my home in the first place. I felt negligent by being oblivious to its lack if integrity. God revealed to me that it was His will that Kloey be returned to Him at that particular time. Nothing that was in my power could have prevented His will to be done. God used that table as a tool, but if there had not been the table, He would have used something else.

I say to any of you struggling with guilt, some things happen to fulfill God's perfect plan. On the same note, I say to you who are placing blame on others that you are listening to Satan's lies to destroy you, your family, or someone you care about. Where is your faith in the Almighty's sovereignty? Jim had seen Kloey swing on the table once before. Neither one of us blames the other for our lack of forethought.

A great loss like ours does one of two things: It can tear a couple apart or it can bond them together. No one else shares the pain with me like Kloey's daddy, and no one else shares my faith as intimately as my husband. It is a blessing to know that it will always be the same person. Our marriage has been fired by high heat like a clay pot. Once the clay has been fired it does not crumble, and because of its new strength the pot can withstand much more rough stuff from life. So can our marriage. To use again the analogy of the branches in John 15:1, they were pruned to allow new life to flourish. The Almighty cut us back so we might see the rawness of our souls. After dreams and expectations are yanked in a blink of an eye, what are left are the truths and the unconditional love of the Lord. We were taken on one of God's field trips so we could best learn this lesson. God is all we really need and should ever depend on.

No longer do I have fear, because I have walked through my worst fear. I live in faith. I stand between His sovereignty and His love. God tells me, "Let the little children come to me. Do not hinder those to come into the kingdom of heaven."

I have peace in knowing Kloey is with the Sovereign God with the perfect plan. Every Christian mother wants that very same thing for her child I am sure; yet the timing is not ours, but the Lord's.

As this time of year rolls around, I can't help but reflect on the state of things in November 2000, when my defining moment occurred. Undoubtedly, the spiritual world was present and accounted for. The final outcome of the presidential election was still unknown at the time of Kloey's accident. The country was unsettled and on edge, waiting for the Lord to show His mighty ways. The financial world seemed to be crumbling as the .com companies were going under, and seemingly successful and brilliant people were losing their jobs.

The Left Behind books about the rapture and the tribulation were on the best-seller list. I had heard these writings were responsible for bringing more people to salvation second only to the Bible.

I never see a chocolate ice cream cone that I don't think of the last snack I made Kloey. She was wearing a cute, lavender, cotton-knit jumper with white polka dots and an embroidered snowman on the front. Big sister Kasey had one to match, and both girls had worn them to the church Thanksgiving dinner. To protect her outfit from the chocolate ice cream that was inevitably about to be drizzled down the front, I quickly slipped it off and flung it to a kitchen chair. I didn't notice at the time, but I must have missed my target. Kloey enjoyed her ice cream on that warm San Antonio November afternoon carefree, wearing only her diaper. The purple and white snowman suit was the last thing she wore.

Upon returning from the hospital in the wee hours of the morning, I had a sick poignant feeling to see her clothes turned inside out and lying where she had been standing. My thoughts turned to the portrayals in the Left Behind books. Believers were raptured up right out of their clothes wherever they were at the time God secretly came. What was really going on in the heavens when Kloey was taken? I know my world was rocked. OK, God, you have my attention! I'm listening!

Chapter 9

As Jesus was sitting on the Mount of Olives, the
disciples came to him privately. "Tell us," they said,
"when will this happen, and what will be the sign of
your coming and of the end of the age?"

—Matt. 24:3

A friend and then business associate of my husband
pointed out to me the unusual sighting of a particular species of an owl in a tree in our yard. The bird
was high up, blending in to the tree by the second-story
children's bedroom window. Of course any owl in a tree
in our developed neighborhood would have been odd.
I dimly recall the owl sighting to be late August, but I
vividly recall its presence for several weeks after that.

I don't like birds anyway, but his haunting demeanor made me uneasy when I was coming and going from the house. I had heard the old superstition that when an owl appears outside your window death is coming for you. The Michael Murphy song from the 70's about the "hoot owl howling outside your window eight nights in a row" played in my head.

Half-joking, half-not, I told Jim about the owl and the superstition behind it. He scolded me for speaking such silly, morbid, and, most of all, nonbiblical beliefs. Jesus told His disciples to watch out so that no one deceives them. Mother Nature, chance, luck...whatever are comfortable labels for the secular world, it's all God!

God has everything at His fingertips to try to reach us. If He has to reach us at some level of familiarity, then that is just what He will do. If you were to try to communicate with an average Korean man on the streets in his native country, you probably would not consider striking up a conversation in French. I liked that familiar Michael Murphy song, and God knew it!

Call it fate. Call it coincidence. Call it destiny. The world calls it such so as not to give any credit to God, for we believers can differentiate in our hearts when God, our Mighty Creator of all, has been at work. God uses many tools. I question not His ways. I do not understand them, I admit. I feel in my heart to this day that He was sending me a sign I might relate to in order to prepare me for what was to come. Was that a winged angel in an owl package? What a disguise! God is all around us, speaking to us in various and often unusual ways. Pray for revelation and the wisdom to be discerning. Stay on your toes!

Chapter 10

Are not all angels ministering spirits sent to serve those who will inherit salvation?

—Hebrews 1:13

Kloey Grace and I would do our grocery shopping at the HEB in the middle of the week. Dad was at work and Kasey at school of course. We would park in the same parking spot every time we went. Before I would get her from her car seat in the back seat, we had a little ritual. I would put my lips on her body and blow raspberries. I would put my face in her face and say, "Where's the baby? Where's the baby?" I would call Kloey my pet name for her, Bitsy Boo.

Across the front, outside the HEB were a series of large heavy cement balls, mainly there for security in blocking vehicles from the area, but designed to be decorative as well. Kloey would test them every time by pushing the big balls to see if today would be the day that the balls would actually roll. She would go down the row and push on almost every one (depending on how much of a hurry we were in that day). To this day on every trip to the grocery store, I still see her there doing her experiment.

The first time I went back to the HEB without her in my cart was an unbearable experience, one of those meltdown moments. With each new aisle I traveled, I saw the snacks that she would want. I heard in my head the things I would normally be saying to her to keep her entertained during her stay in the shopping cart. Unfortunately, there was no need today to snap it up and get done before her patience in shopping ran out. I thought my tears were going to erupt with screams as loud as a wild animal. I had a feeling like my body wanted to start shaking.

Just then, I rounded the corner of yet another aisle, and there was Martha. I knew her face from that ladies' retreat that God made me go on back in October. She organized the ladies' ministry at our church too. I looked familiar to her as well. "Hi, how are you?" she asked. Of course, I had no choice but to answer truthfully in the state that I was in. And just "how I was" came pouring out! Do you know she prayed boldly with me right there in the middle of the aisle at the HEB. I know that all the hustle and bustle of the Saturday morning shoppers did not go away, but for those minutes, Martha, God, and I were the only ones in the HEB that morning. God is right where you need Him!

I finished up and tearfully made it back home. What did His angel look like in this encounter? Well, a lot like a church lady pushing a grocery cart!

I have to tell you, to this day, no matter how crowded the HEB parking lot is, that space that Kloey and I always parked in is always open for me and memories of my Bitsy Boo. I park there almost every time. That space acts as a tape measure of how God has brought me to the place He has me today. I could barely walk across the parking lot to those big balls soon after Kloey left us, and now I can do so to the glory of God.

Several weeks later I went on a shopping trip again to a furniture store. My angel of a girlfriend, Linda, went with me. She had been with me or at least called me every day since Kloey left us, and three months later she even bought the house next door to me, partially to keep an eye on me and partially because it was a great house with a lot of potential. She was also an interior designer, so for more reasons than one, she was good to have along in a furniture store!

After my HEB experience, I think she and others thought it was not a good idea to have me out in public by myself. I was one of those "others." The world seemed to be going on like nothing had happened. I felt so different inside. Didn't I look different as well? Couldn't the world see that something dreadful had happened? Why were they all going on with business as usual? Why was everyone so caught up in their stuff? Can you believe those people were even smiling and laughing?

Our purpose for furniture shopping was to find replacement furniture for the entry room where the fatal table had been. Kloey's urn was sitting on the center of the rug where the pedestal table had been. It was surrounded by plants, flowers, cards, and all sorts of things that friends had brought to honor Kloey. It was quite a shrine. I was in search of the right thing to put her urn on in that room, a daunting task at best.

Linda and I were shopping on our knees, no pun intended. We were pulling on the tabletops as a child would from their height to test the stability of the pieces. I was appalled at how the marketplace had disregarded child safety when it came to the "tippy-toppiness" of tables. Even though we explained our shopping habits, the salesperson seemed a bit indifferent and unwilling to provide a solution.

A few days later Jim and I set out on our own search for an urn-holding table. Jim hates to shop, but he did it for me, and we both needed a diversion on which to focus. A salesperson quickly approached us, as salespeople always do when working on commission. We briefly told her we needed a table for a front room. She walked with us through the store showing us a few ominous-looking tables. At that point, we clarified the circumstance for the need for the table and what it would be used for.

I was only a stranger to her, but suddenly we had a connection. She began to tell me of the loss of her teenage son, who was killed in a car accident many years ago. Her pain was still very evident. I thought, *after nearly twenty years, will it still hurt for me too? Would God be able to heal me? Will I ever be the same?* I believe I know the answers to those questions now: yes, yes, no! God revealed to me that I will always be emotional when I speak of my sweet Kloey and the circumstances that God used to mold us.

If there ever came a day when my heart was not full of such passion, then that is the day I am useless for the Lord. I shall not wait to give my testimony when I can speak without tears. There will be no day. It's real, it's fiery, and I'm to use it for the Lord's glory.

Whether it was a generational trait, a religious belief, or the way she and her family chose to deal with their situation, the lady in the furniture store had not been able to talk about her son. They had brushed the incident under the rug and attempted the best they could to live in denial about their loss. That was not my style! We had to keep Kloey's name alive in our conversations to honor her short life and to keep her personal details from being forgotten.

Our conversation quickly became intimate, and we knew right away we were both women of great faith. She asked if I would pray with her and so I did. My husband looked on as we had our mommy prayer time. Was I being used as her angel that day? "Me, Lord?"

I wish that I had been in a stronger place of my own to better minister to her, but God is in control and I am sure He gave her what she needed. She was able to give me what I needed. The woman, through God, revealed to me that I must find strength to pass on the ministering that was passed to me. Wow! God is in the stores too!

> "Do not forget to entertain strangers, for by so do- ing some people have entertained angels without knowing it."
>
> —Heb. 13:2

Chapter 11

It is better to go to a house of mourning than to go to a house of feasting, for death is the destiny of every man; the living should take this to heart.

—Ecclesiastes 7:2

It was early October 2000 when my aunt passed away. For as long as I was old enough to be aware, she had health concerns. I did not see any change in her health, so her passing did come as a surprise to me.

Her funeral was graveside in East Texas on an unusually cold, rainy, and blustery, Columbus Day weekend. Our family had reservations with two other families at a condo on the beaches of Port Aransas, Texas. Of course, I chose to fly up to be with my extended family. I sent Kasey and Jim on to the beach (we did not know about the bad weather at this time). I took Kloey with me and planned to fly back after the service to meet up with the others at the coast. We did not feel we were ready just yet to explain the reality of death and what happens at a burial to Kasey. Most of my extended family had not met Kloey, so I was compelled to bring her with me. She was young, so she did not really understand what had happened. This was a good plan, one I do not regret.

The heavens were not rejoicing on this day in early October. The sky was gray and the wind was angry. The clouds were crying down rain, and the air had an old smell like that of a place that is mostly left to nature. The churchyard visually read like pages from a history book. The massive headstones were from a time lost, but if you were still in doubt, you just had to check the dates on the grave markers.

This is the first time Kloey had worn a coat. I put her red Polartec swing coat with purple bows down the front on her as we got out of the car at the blustery old churchyard. She wanted the coat off! It was making her cold! She never had been cold like this when she wasn't wearing this coat. What a concept. What a funny memory.

As the service for my Aunt Nonnette began, the family huddled under the tent to keep warm and be protected from the rain. The pastor began to speak, and a beautiful letter from her granddaughter was read. I was standing next to my uncle and my sister, holding a rather squirmy Kloey. God began to speak to me. My mind strayed from the audible words that were being spoken in the huddle to words that were meant only for me. I would be attending another funeral for someone under this tent in the very near future. It was a prophetic, yet upsetting, magnification of an already tough time. With a lump in my throat and tears in my eyes, I began scanning the faces under the tent. "Lord, is it to be my uncle, who is a heart patient? Is it to be my mom, who is the oldest of her siblings?" It was never in my realm of thinking that it would be the youngest under that tent, the very one I was holding, my very own baby. Never was that a consideration.

Jehovah Shammah, the Lord is there, and He is the ultimate teacher. Again, I am no scholar of prophecy, but if I had had my spiritual telescope I could have zoomed in on what was to take place a month and a half later. The great Teacher was preparing me with a vision beyond my immediacy by using where I was at the moment to prepare me for a place I would go in the future. Just as Christ used parables to teach in the Scriptures, He also uses this telescopic method to teach of forthcoming events using former events.

I can say it is life-confirming to be a student of the Lord. How worthy I feel to be used by Him. He has chosen me. I am His vessel. I am His tool. For what? You know, I don't really care. I will go wherever He takes me. I am thankful for not connecting the dots to my defining moment. To grasp the devastation of what was to come would have been unbearable. So you see, sometimes we don't need to know everything. Receive it as God sends it!

After returning home, I knew I was going to be put in a position to explain death to my children. The Lord had made it clear in my head and heart that He was ready to take someone else that was under that family tent very soon. Our relatives were aging and some had failing health. Kasey was really who I felt I needed to prepare by teaching her about loss. Kloey was still too young at twenty months to be concerned with such a topic, so I set out to find age-appropriate material for Kasey.

I went to Amazon.com and bought Maria Shriver's children's book about what happens when people die. The book came two weeks before the reality of loss hit our home. Yes, I had the book, but the circumstances were drastically different than I ever expected or could have possibly foreseen, in spite of having the greatest Teacher ever.

Not many things shape us or define us more than how we handle a struggle in our lives. All eyes were on us after Kloey left us. The emotional ball, so to speak, was in our court. The way people reacted to us was a result of how we were going to embrace our God-given situation. Were we going to be at constant odds with our Maker for what He had taken from us? We knew a lady who, after losing her college-age daughter in a car accident, now stood a little too close to the ledge for most folks' comfort level, if you know what I mean. She needed prescription drugs to get her through the day. Her therapist was at a point of having no solutions to offer. "'Where was God?" you ask. Oh, He was right there offering help that was never accepted.

It is here at this place of ultimate struggle when our friends either respect and admire the glory of God being shown through us or discover things about us that we wish they didn't know. I tell you, struggle through your crisis with God and you'll reach a personal place of glory in the Lord. You'll be blessed, shaped, and redefined beyond your human understanding. There is no better testimony for the Lord than for others to witness firsthand how the Lord renews a once broken spirit to produce fruit that gives glory to the Lord.

Chapter 12

All the days ordained for me were written in your book before one of them came to be.

—Psalm 139:16

It's the week of Christmas that I am writing. There will not be a Christmas that I don't wonder what Kloey would've asked Santa to bring her. I see perfume bottles so finely displayed in the stores, ready for holiday gift giving, and wonder which one I would've chosen for Kloey's collection this year. Her small collection adorns the shelf in her room with John 12:3: "Then Mary took about a twelve-ounce jar of expensive perfume made from the essence of nard, and she anointed Jesus' feet with her hair. And the house was filled with the fragrance of the perfume." By the way, I don't think you can call it a coincidence that this verse was the theme of the women's retreat—the same one that I was in protest of attending. God was teaching me to be more of a Mary than the Martha that I had been, especially where Kloey Grace was concerned. Our home is filled with the fragrance of what Kloey brought to our lives and with what gifts she left us.

Allow your fragrance to float out and unto the heavens. Release your fragrance so others can inhale the sweet smell. Be fragrant for the Lord!

I've received Christmas cards from friends with pictures of children that are Kloey's "would be" age this season. For the lack of being able to explain the emotion, I say I feel a bit perplexed that they have grown and my baby will stay twenty-one months forever in my mind. It is a strange measuring stick with which to be associated.

Only when Satan inserts himself do I think of the trauma of the accident. Through God, I only allow myself the sweet memories of Kloey and her short life. It is a struggle to keep out and refuse thoughts of her cold, lifeless body. When my mind plays that videotape of the accident back to me, I know that it is Satan messing with me. I rebuke him in the name of Jesus. Together Jesus and I can have victory over the Devil.

Like most moms do, I touch my children who live with me while they lie still and sleeping. I'm sure most mothers do not notice or appreciate the warmth that they feel from their bodies, the smell of life they exude, or the feel of moisture under their flesh. My experience has allowed me to appreciate that we are all just a breath away from death. Death is not a faraway place at all. Truly, we are just a breath away. One minute lively, and the next all has been altered.

We attended worship services at our old congregation that November day that redefined my life. Following the service, we had a wonderful time of fellowship with our friends at the annual church family Thanksgiving dinner. This celebration was our reason for returning to visit our previous church home. We had the traditional foods of celebration. Kloey was blessed by a very festive last meal surrounded by all the folks who were in attendance at her baptismal service on Mother's Day the prior year.

After the Thanksgiving celebration, we had planned to do some yard work back home to meet the deadline for the semiannual curbside brush pick-up scheduled for the upcoming week. Jim needed to trim our trees, so I scheduled myself to be outside too. I joked with Jim and a neighbor passing by, "I'm not out here to help, just to call 911 when he falls off the ladder!" I did end up calling 911 that day for the first time in my life, but, as you know, it wasn't because Jim fell off his ladder. During the course of tree trimming, Kloey had sneaked nearly to the top of that ladder while no one was looking. If she were to have fallen, it would have severely injured or even killed her. I spotted her before her adventuresome spirit got her in trouble, but it still made her mother's heart fly up to her throat. I wonder if the angels were about to take her then.

It was a bit early to put silk poinsettias in the pots, I admit, but since I was hanging out to be the safety patrol anyway, I decided to make the most of my time and multitask. I had taken the spring/fall silks out of the planters, and Kasey was playing with them. I will never forget her comment as she took the flowers and stuck them in the ground by a big tree, "I'm putting flowers on my dead sister's grave." I scolded her for playing such a gruesome game. "It makes me sad to think of something like that, so I don't want you to play that," I said.

Not only did this thought make me sad, I was surprised at Kasey's statement. We had held back on the concept of burial. We had visited a military cemetery with her before, where Grandma Betty lay, but we termed the headstones "memorial markers" to honor those in heaven. We did not introduce the fact that bodies were underground and the memorial markers were the headstones. I had my new Maria Shriver book from Amazon, but we had not read it to her yet. We had taught Kasey that heaven was up in the clouds and hell was underground. Now how were we going to explain godly people being put under the ground when they go meet Jesus? Yes, I was shocked to hear the words coming from her mouth.

Chapter 12

Apparently, our kindergartener Kasey knew more about this subject than we thought. Now upon reflection, I realize those words were not her words but words from God. Nothing could have prepared me for what was to come later that day, but I have to wonder if God was opening my mind to the unimaginable.

Chapter 13

During the night the mystery was revealed to Daniel in a vision. Then Daniel praised God of heaven and said:

Praise be to the name of God for ever and ever;
Wisdom and power are his.
He changes times and seasons;
He sets up kings and deposes them.
He gives wisdom to the wise
and knowledge to the discerning.
He reveals deep and hidden things;
He knows what lies in darkness,
And light dwells with him.
I thank and praise you, O God of my father:

You have given me wisdom and power,
You have made known to us the dream of the
king.

—Daniel 2:19–23

In my sleep I have only dreamed about Kloey once. It eerily seems that God has a purpose for not allowing her to come to me as I sleep. Go figure! I dream about other things that seem so insignificant. Kloey is such a big part of me, and yet I do not have dreams of her. Well, only once, as I mentioned, and the dream was clear and as real as everyday live action. Where is Daniel the dream interpreter when you need him!

Kloey was a regular in the church nursery on Sunday mornings. She always accepted getting dropped off, but when she would see us through the viewing window or at the counter to pick her up, she would race to us with open arms in excitement so glad to see us and ready to go home.

In my dream, we were watching her play on the indoor little slide and play equipment. She was having much fun, smiling and laughing with the other children. Kloey looked up briefly to see that we were there watching. In the dream, not only did she not rush to us, she did not even interrupt her play or pause her happy giggles. We reached our arms toward her, but she would not come. Her attention was 100 percent elsewhere.

I believe God was saying to me that she is very happy with Him in the playground of heaven. She does not long for me as I long for her. Jesus is with her in all her contentment. God gives me no subsequent validation through more dreams. He showed me once, and now I need to draw upon my faith in His promise.

I believe God likes to do something once, and check it off His list so as not to have to do it again. He knows I'm all about that, too! We get baptized once for all time, and He sacrificed His Son once for all time. It's something that doesn't wear off or need to be reapplied or recharged like a camera battery.

Kloey is joyful with her Lord for all time in a glorious place, and if I never have another night vision, I can be OK with that. So you see, we'd better listen because sometimes God says things only once!

Chapter 14

Children are a gift from the Lord.

—Psalm 127:3

As I mentioned earlier, both Kasey and Kloey were invitro fertilization (IVF) babies from frozen embryos. For those of you not in the know, in a nutshell, this is a fertility process where my eggs are extracted, fertilized by Jim's sperm, and implanted in my uterus. I make it sound simple, but there are a lot of expensive injections and other drugs used to get the multiple eggs for extraction and the uterus primed for receiving an implant. It is not a procedure; it is a process and is very costly. Not just costly in terms of finances—it certainly is that—but costly too in terms of emotional stress and physical pain. The exorbitant amount of hormones being received into the body is enough to cause anyone to hang over the edge a bit. At the time, the T-shirt that jokes "I'm on estrogen and I've got a gun" seemed a bit too close to reality to be funny.

All joking aside, IVF is a stressful process to embark upon even in the best of circumstances. Bottom line, it is not easy for us to get pregnant.

Two weeks after Kloey left us, Kasey asked if "we" could have another baby. She was part of the "we," as she was missing her sister too. Her request hit us in a strange sort of way, as if that was what God wanted us to do. We also knew that nothing and no one could replace Kloey Grace. Then my thoughts went to the difficulty of the process.

"Good idea, Kasey." It sounded simple enough from a babe's mouth.

As wild as it sounded and emotional as I was, we felt God had spoken those words through Kasey. Immediately, we began the process. On the first try of IVF, I was pregnant. It was four years ago this week that we found out the pregnancy was a tubal pregnancy, and the tube was about to rupture. I had surgery to remove the tube and to tie off the other so it would not happen again. It was the second time this rare occurrence for an IVF patient happened.

I don't want to dismiss the grief that comes from a miscarriage, but this setback just rolled right off me. I had experienced the sobs of death and the pain from a debilitating grief. I had held death in my arms.

I was so certain God would deliver a promise of another child to our family that I walked right through this trial with faith wrapped around my shoulders. This was a mere stumbling block that was used for a stepping stone. My perspective was that this was a light and momentary space in the kingdom's plan. I had peace about the whole process because I was so into the Lord during this time and, you know, He was so into me too. I was the best when my relationship with Him was based on such dependence. It's true, because I was weak, I was strong. I was totally His during these times. I want to cling to that kind of relationship for always and every day, whether my life is at a peak or I'm walking through a valley. I have been through fertility treatment when my life was full of hopes for a future of fulfilled dreams, and I have been there tense with grief. The ease of the process and the peace about the outcome was the strongest during the latter. I pray that you can receive my testimony and apply it to your own circumstances.

As soon as I healed we began the process again. As I said, no one can stop the pain of losing a child, but refocusing on another baby sure did help all three of us. We were not strangers to reattempts with IVF.

Though we prepared ourselves for several more attempts, the next procedure resulted in another pregnancy. God would deliver on a promise to me in nine months. "The secret things belong to the Lord our God, but the things revealed belong to us and to our children forever, that we may follow all the words of the law" (Deut. 29:29).

On my fortieth birthday I was having the best party anyone could ever have—a *baby shower*!! Kerby Faith Wickens was born February 6, 2002, just four days before Kloey's birthday.

I must mention that Kerby and Kloey had exactly the same due dates, February 14, Saint Valentine's Day. I am sure this is God's way of lifting our spirits at a time we might otherwise have been consumed with thoughts of what might have been. Instead we were rejoicing in what the Lord has delivered us through. Big sister Kasey was deeply thrilled with the arrival of Kerby. She was as complete and satisfied as she could be in what would always be an imperfect and incomplete earthly family. We all were right there with her in her bliss!

Other middle names for Kerby were considered, but my friend Linda told me that it was our faith that got us to this place, so Kerby's middle name should be Faith. This was undeniably true, so Faith it is! Kerby means "follower of God." Wait until she is old enough to understand how God brought her to us. She will surely live up to her name. God has big plans for Kerby, as we feel He really wanted her here. What a gift from God! The road of grieving certainly would have been so much longer and rougher had it not been for Kerby.

Our biblical sister Sarah died in her grand old age. Her son, Isaac, extremely close to his mother, was comforted by someone God put in his life. God sent Rebekah to Isaac as his wife. Kerby is my Rebekah. She gave hope and happiness to our family. We began to breathe again. I began to sing in church again. There was always joy to be had in the Lord, but now I began to feel joy and even feel happiness, something I thought I had lost for eternity. We, as good stewards, may choose to send flowers or cook a meal as a gift to show our condolences. God sent Kerby! He is a God who does things in a big way, you know, because He can.

Epilogue

Blessed are those who hear the word of God and obey it.

—Luke 11:28

There is that story where the man drives his expensive car down the same street every evening after work on his way home. One day a boy hits the side of the car with a brick, and it does obvious damage to the Jag. The man gets out and angrily questions the boy as to his motives. The boy replies, "I am here every day and you never noticed me. I wanted you to see me." I hope I don't have to spell it out that the boy is the voice of the Lord. If I do, you'd better watch out for flying bricks!

I have shared my personal testimony with you of some times when the Spirit has shown Himself to me.

Sometimes the Lord puts the words in someone else's mouth to be spoken out. He uses unlikely people today as He has done throughout history.

Whatever your situation, the Holy Spirit is there to guide you. It is up to you to receive the Spirit into your heart, and certainly it's your choice to be responsive. Find out what God's will for your life is. You don't know what you are missing if you are not being receptive. Are you listening?

It pleases the Lord that we read His written word, the Bible. It also pleases Him for us to pray without ceasing. This is called communication—He speaks to us; we speak to Him. You form a personal relationship with your Lord. He wants us to worship Him and to know Him in a personal way. I believe He cares little for preprinted prayers and rituals made by people. It's not business. It's personal! That is why prayer is so important. What would your relationship be like with your spouse, children, friends, or co-workers if you had very little communication?

You build a relationship the same, whether it is earthly or heavenly. There is no difference. Build a marriage with God. Build a relationship. Connect! Let Him speak to you. You speak to Him. That's the way it works.

I hope you've concluded on your own, through your reading, that we can't totally be filled up with God when we are carrying other stuff inside. I want to close by reminding you to let go of your stuff and give it to God. Be led by the Spirit of God. You aren't driving the bus. Surrender it all. Let the Lord drive your bus! Empower yourself through God. Be weak so you may be strong through the Lord.

Did the Lord give you talents and gifts you are not using as He intends? What does the Lord want from you? Are you just taking and not giving glory to the Lord as fitting to His plan? Wherever you are in your faith, I hope you go forth challenged. Never stop seeking understanding of the Holy Spirit.

Can you picture God with His big megaphone, trying to get your attention? I put my hands on your shoulders out of love right now, and I shake you.

Wake up!!

Listen!

Grow in your faith! God is speaking to *you*! Trust me, you don't want God to do the shaking.

Comments and inquires are welcomed and
encouraged by the author.

http://kellywickens.authorweblog.com/

To order additional copies of this title call:
1-877-421-READ (7323)
or please visit our Web site at
www.pleasantwordbooks.com

If you enjoyed this quality custom-published book,
drop by our Web site for more books and information.

www.winepressgroup.com
"Your partner in custom publishing."

LaVergne, TN USA
10 November 2009
163688LV00001B/17/A